ADAM'S CHOICE

JOHN MOFFITT

ADAM'S CHOICE

The Golden Quill Press
PUBLISHERS
Francestown   New Hampshire

Acknowledgment

"Fire Sacrifice" originally appeared in *Quixote*. The interpolated passages from Mundaka Upanishad I. ii and II. i are adapted from the Nikhilananda translation, and they are used with the kind permission of Harper & Row. The quotation from Louis Macneice's "Autumn Journal," at the head of "Take Heart," is reproduced with the kind permission of Random House, New York.

Contents

I

FIRE SACRIFICE

The angel stood by the gate
Smooth shut and bolted fast
   On paradise just lost,
And the flaming sword he held upraised
In his peremptory hand
   Lustily crackled, hissed,
     Doom-fanned,
Till every other sound fell mute
And all the air about
     Spoke with the single sound.

Too late aroused, too late
Repenting what they ate,
   And drugged now with the fragrant fruit,
Our tricked foreparents turned,
As the flames hissed and burned,
   And eastward out of Eden
Took their hesitant way
Into the unrevealing light
     Of ordinary day.

(This is the truth: the ritual works revealed
To the seers, all of which are set down in the sacred
     hymns,
Are variously expounded in the threefold Veda:
Perform them, eager to earn their certain fruits.
This is the highway leading to your rites' fruition.)

Now first our parents looked again,
Hopeful, in one another's face
    And saw, dejected, then
A darkness clouding either one,
While on their hampered flesh
    Hung garments of secretiveness;
And gazing backward toward
Where the stern guardian stood,
    Saw still that blade of warning flame
        Luring and menacing
    Before the eastern gate,
Bearing fierce witness there
To the brief wonder they had known.

Amidst the clamor of their pride and shame,
        Remembering
All they had known, had been —
Finding it now painted, in a dream,
    Darkly outside of them —
    And tracing no way back
To the quick Presence and the Light
    That once pervaded them
    In that unclouded state,
Restless, our foreparents pressed onward now
    From the accusing gate,
        Dreaming one day to reattain
        The abandoned seat.

(When the fire is kindled well
And the lifting flames are flickering strong,
Let a man forthwith offer his oblation
In the space midway between the northern and southern
parts of the fire.)

2

. . . And came to the Elder Bard,
Past Sumer, Memphis, blazing Knossos, came —
    Remembering —
To where the Bat-blind One,
Strongest of all our elder singers, sat
   Singing of waters, keels and men,
Singing in dactyls and iambs
The destinies of men
    And the churned Ionian sea;
Past Sparta came, to helmed Athene's home,
   Where in the market walked
   That other Ancient One —
That irresistible, homely man —
With his two striving sons,
   Who compassed all men's thoughts
   In their two striving brains.

And the clean column shapes,
   Measured and strong,
Beat back the beating light,
The light chimerical
    That hovered over all.

13

(Now, if his offering is unsupported
By supplementary rites and by hospitality,
Or if his rites are heedlessly performed
Or the oblations offered at an improper moment,
Then perish all his hopes in the seven worlds.)

And crossing two bold files of tumbled hills
Between which rolled a sky-stained sea,
    Straightway our parents came,
    Deep in the watching grove,
On the twin sons of Rhea's womb
    Pulling at the loose paps
    Of her, the hairy dam,
Whose dumb compassion warmly nursed
       Their infant thirst;
Turned now and heard the tramp of marshaled men
    Pound the white pavements, echo from
    The arches of aspiring Rome;
Saw the Dictator rise
    And manners and the law extend
    Around the vine-trimmed shores,
Fattened on gold and blood and auguries;

Looked then, again, in one another's face —
    Remembering —
And saw, perplexed,
Two rigid masks of loneliness;
    And all the light was gone
    That earlier shone from them,
And pride of will was written deeply there.

Now suddenly they came, in a still town
      At the remotest end
      Of that well-ordered realm,
Upon the desolate inn
      Where in the winter's night
      The red rose, blossoming,
The seed of Jesse's line,
         Blossomed and shone;
Passed onward up the hill
Toward the Place of the Skull,
      Where now the bleeding rose,
            Full-blown,
Bare, nerveless hung,
Weighed with the world's weight,
      Before the wing-hid throne;
And as the life took wing
      They heard Gehenna's fire
      Speak on the thunder's tongue.

And silently our parents watched as bands
Of serene martyrs, saints and celebrants,
         In apostolic faith,
      Spread the hushed word abroad
      Of a new-risen Lord,
And holy fathers, in forewarning zeal,
      From council hall and cell
Shepherded the majestic march
         Of a redeeming Church;
Then, as they still pressed on,
Through hanging, tree-shot mist

In twilight gloom along the Appenines
Watched the last licking flames
Quietly branch about the ruined shrines
      And the swift night crouch down.

(Kāli, Karāli, Manojavā: black, terrifying, swift-as-
      thought,
Sulohita, Sudhumravarnā: quick-red, smoke-purple-
      bright,
Sphulingini: spark-thrown,
And Visvaruchi: gleaming-every-formed —
These seven, thus flickering, compose
The seven tongues of the sacrificial fire.)

3

Back on the wide East now our parents gazed
Toward the One Prophet, where unhindered grew
    The kingdoms of his progeny,
    And as the dark rolled on,
Watched his bold crescent reach and spread its claw
Like a huge crab's, to crush all Christendom;
    Saw it, dispersed, recede at last
    To the bare African coast;
Watched then responding waves
    Of papal pride and power
Push to reclaim the Holy Sepulcher.

Onward now pressed those two —
    Remembering —

Through the vast, dim-lit airs
Of reaching naves and storied choirs,
Through workshops, courts and schools;
    Saw Francis climb and cling
  In mute, adoring humbleness
  To the high, threatening cross
And take the Seraph's harsh embrace;
  Heard, too, amidst the wars
Of princes, Dante, hailing heaven's King,
  Invoke hell's paralyzing pangs
  On souls self-wrapt from grace
Or, for the erring, purgatory's banishment
    From the Eternal Face,
And hymn the ordered joy of paradise;

  While plague and hunger and mischance
  Ravaged a fumbling populace,
Watched a new Hellas, quickened into flame,
  Under closed, clouded skies
  Fan its exploring blaze
    From Italy to France,
Then, all at once,
Saw that great fire race down the kindled aisles
  Of her that nourished it
    And mock its nourisher.

(He who makes offering while the flames are gleaming
And pours oblations at the preordered hour
Is borne with them on the fanning rays of the sun

To where abides the shining gods' sole sovereign.
To him the bright oblations cry: "Come hither! Come
    hither!"
And lead him on the rays of the sun,
Worshiping him all the while and greeting him
Thus pleasantly: "This is the holy heaven
Your goodly works have earned.")

. . . Looked now, again, in one another's face
    And saw, aghast,
On either one the visage of the Beast,
And on each brow, corrupting all their grace,
    A pall of greed and wretchedness;
Watched the slow octopus of empire swell
    Along the westward coast,
And swifter now uncurling, stretch and flail
    Its cupped and sucking arms
    About two hemispheres;

Saw Leonardo, pondering
Values, designs and distances,
    Unveil the future's potencies;
Heard Luther's wrath assail
The money-changers in the outer court,
    Then saw him swerve
    And with his cohorts move
    Into a new apostasy;
Heard the maimed Church reply
And watched Ignatius steer her shaken steps
    Toward the dim Orient coast;

Saw all Spain founder in the wrestling wake
      Of the Armada's wreck,
And Europe, buffeted and lost,
   Labor distractedly
   Through an enormous sea
Roiled deep by controversial winds
And tides of sedulous intrigue
      And fratricidal wars.

(But frail and easily wrecked are those sacrficial rafts
Steered by the sixteen priests and the two votaries,
On which the lesser worship rests:
Fools who esteem them for the highest good
Shall bow again and again to age and death.)

. . . And as they waited there —
      Remembering —
Heard then the Seer of Avon ardently
   Invoke the ancient Name
That burns unquenchable beneath
Time's waste, beneath these busy lusts of men,
   And in a tongue inflamed
   Shape the taut English tongue;
Heard Milton, after him,
   Recall for flagging men
Their great Taskmaster's rigorous ways
And justify his unrelenting purposes;
   Saw rapt Spinoza calculate
      Creation's theorem
And plot the Godhead reaching though all things;

Saw Newton, titan-brained,
    Astride his fresh-won world of light
    Trace the mechanics of the skies;

Heard then arise
The firm, prophetic voice
    Of Bach, which out of ages wrung
    A mighty surge of measured tone
To set a smouldering seal
    On crowded harmonies to come;
And watched as Kant,
    Charting his two-fold world
    Of timeless essences and timeward forms,
Calmly surveyed a fevered continent
    Racked yet with wasting wars
    And boiling fierce, at last,
        Into rebellion's ecstasies.

(So, witless children, wrapt in manifold error,
Flatter themselves to have seized life's final good:
Because these votaries of ritual works,
Desire-led, fail to achieve the truth,
They fall from heaven, misery-struck,
When the ripened fruits of their works are spent.)

4

. . . Watched one more daring than the rest descend,
Beethoven, proud and pitying,
    Bearing the live Promethean brand,

To seize the boisterous soul
Of revolution's better part,
　　And while an Emperor
　　Was courted, crowned and cursed,
Weaving a vision of the hero's will,
　　　　Hymning the chastened heart.

Our foreparents heard, then,
　　Above the bite of whips
　　And bickering of ineffectual men,
Compassionate Lincoln, harassed and alone,
　　In words of searching flame
Invoke again the saving Name,
Which none would stop to hear
　　But all men clamored down
In a new world's frenetic rush
To wrest the prize of world-eclipsing power;
　　Saw Darwin, unawares,
　　Hearten its purposes,
Tracing the protoplasmic urge
That spawns, as if with fixed intent,
　　New and superior forms to meet
　　The challenge of their element;
Looked close as Freud now subtly probed
　　In the sick, naked self,
The mazes of subliminal night,
And Einstein ranged upon his thought
　　Far as the web of space-and-time's
　　Expanding verge
Or inward dived to the veiled atom's void;

Stared into the world's womb, where, warped with fear,
   A maddened mood began to breed;
   Saw the fierce swirl of war
Draw the distracted nations in
   Toward its devouring core,
And Marx's dialectic urge,
Tuned to a restless proletariat,
   Spanning an unresponsive age
   Reach out to invade
The groping minds of sicklier days
      Amidst the groans of dynasties;
Heard the new Caesars lift their bloated cry,
   Saw half the world obey;
Watched war's slow wave heap up and burst again,
   And at the embattled Tower
   Saw the red fire-bombs rain
      The last of empires down
      Into immense oblivion;
Saw rise the mushroom cloud
      Out of the flash of doom.

(But wiser souls, of tranquil mind,
Who in the forest find slim sustenance on alms,
Practicing penance fitted to their station
And meditating on the world's Creator —
They, cleansed, depart by the Path of Light
To the high sphere where dwells the deathless Supreme
      Person.)

Now from that lesser hell
Our foreparents moved on —
     Remembering —
Toward the last marge of time,
Toward this thin, flame-licked ledge we cling upon,
    And from it heard
A world plagued with unease, confused, and torn
Between obsessive creeds and purposes,
    Amidst the drone of ravening machines
    And blast of rockets and hurled satellites
Fling its harsh taunt and cry
     Back at the fabled Source
     It cannot quite dismiss:

    "Blind Force!
If you be, oh, at all,
    Your Presence shrinks so far
    From where we are,
From our precise concerns,
    That no ear, not even yours,
Could catch our echoes for the gulf between;
    The sword your angel once held high
    Now veils its hissing fire
And flares unseen —
Yes, if it flares at all;
    Therefore we have no need
For other faith than the bleak-eyed
Resourcefulness to live and strive,
    The candid courage but to be."

(Let a true votary, after pondering well
All those wide worlds that ritual works and prayer
bestow,
Divest himself of barren-wombed desire:
From that which perishes, that which is imperishable
cannot spring.
If he would know the imperishable truth,
Let him, fuel in hand,
Seek out a teacher versed in the spirit of the Veda
And given to direct contemplation of Brahman.)

5

. . . Came then, at length, and stood
Between that chasm and the long, wide,
Dim-stretching prospect of the tangled past —
    Their adolescence and their adulthood —
    And, startled, saw the whole
Slow, circuitous, but yet inevitable
    Passage from their fall
    To this last pitiful Now:
Saw suddenly, where they stood,
    The whole vague multitude
Of fools and heroes, harpies, flies and men
    Lighted with tongues of flame,
Stuff of their own sheer stuff,
Marked with their own hid name,
      The Name of Everyman;
    Saw that the source of fire
    Was where they were
And only in it was their power;

Looked now, assured, in one another's face
And saw the cloud withdrawn
    That, frowning and impervious,
    Had hung so long before,
And caught the fresh-born light
      Of innocence there.

(This is the truth: as from a blazing fire
Fly sparks in thousands like to it in substance,
So too, O worthy one, fly forth all creatures from the
      imperishable Brahman
And unto him at last return.
He is the self-enlightened Formless Being,
Who, uncaused, everywhere exists — within and
      without all things.)

Decending from that haggard height
To a smooth, sky-girt plain
    Close by the joining limbs
Of Jordan's and of elder Ganga's flood,
    Our foreparents stood then
In quietude and whole contentedness;
    Saw walking near the shore
    A fire-wed pair,
Mirror and image of themselves
For generations yet to come,
    Lotus and rose made one,
Exampling for the rest of time
Chaste union blossomed out of love,
    Their incorruptible faith

Renewed in the new life,
By the joined, shining waves
    With upraised hands
Blessing mankind and beckoning
All men to enter
    Into their blessedness.

(The heavens are his head, the sun and moon his eyes,
The four crosswise directions are his ears,
The revealed Veda is his speech,
The wind his breath, the universal mind his heart;
From his feet the earth was born;
He is, indeed, the inner self of every creature.
O worthy one, whoever beholds this vast, deathless
        Brahman
Hid in the heart's close cave
Severs the knot of old unwisdom here and now.)

. . . Came then and stood beside them on the shore;
Quit of their pride and shame
Came and cast off their clothes,
    The clothes of adulthood;
Bathed in that mingled flood
Flowing serene and bright,
    And saw, high over them,
The clear heavens open and the dove descend;

Looked then, once more, in one another's face
    And saw, unmasked,

The ancient, unborn Face,
The Face of Everyman,
Which, never needing, never asked
   To be unmasked —
   Though to their erring sense
It seemed, from Eden, to have quite withdrawn
Its Presence and its Light from them —
   But still uncomprehended shone
   Where it had always been
Waiting to ease their wilfulness;

Turned now and saw, across the shining flood,
   The angel's flaming brand,
   No longer raised and menacing
      But pointing them beyond
To the remembered gate and Eden found.

THE YOUNG DAVID

Then the young David came and stood
Fronting the warrior multitude,
The Lord being with him. Sober-eyed
He glanced about, as he surveyed
The ragged valley stretched between
His own and the Philistines' men,
Where in unwarming winter sun
He saw Goliath's great hulk ranged
Against their line, his stance unchanged
From the first hour he challenged them
That day to send their man to him;
And saw too the harsh bearded face
Dark with the fury of his race,
Saw how upon his massive head
Down which black locks spilled at the side
He wore a helmet of smart brass,
How all his swelling torso was
Sheathed in a gleaming coat of mail,
And from his waist there hung a steel
Scabbard three full cubits long,
And greaves of brass were on each shin
And round each forearm's swarthy skin
Circled a shining broad brass ring;
Saw how his spearhead's pointed gleam
Budded upon a straight spear stem
Tall as a heavy weaver's beam,
While just before him on the field

A slave stood, set to lift and wield
The weight of his tremendous shield.
And David yet was watching there,
And as he pondered, his head bare
To the unruly winter air,
He looked defiance at the man
Who for long forty days in vain
Sued Israel for a champion.
But Saul, whose fortitude had quailed
After old Samuel first assailed
His waywardness — and, as he went
From the king's presence, took and rent
His mantle's skirt for a sure sign
The Lord's power no more dwelt with him —
Gazed now in wonder at the youth,
Who fearless stood against the uncouth
Defender of the opposing horde,
Half doubting still, even though he heard
From his own lips how David scored
Over a lion's and bear's power
When they had come, one evil hour,
And seized a grown sheep from his flock:
Unarmed even with a shepherd's crook
He caught each by the beard and slew
Them each — and so he would do now
For this uncircumsized lout who
So long had challenged and decried
The armies of the living God.

But the great-limbed Goliath smiled,
And spat, to see a callow child
Run there before him, as if mad,
To succor his vile Hebrew Lord,
And mocking him he raised his voice
Against the Israelites' queer choice,
Standing as yet quite unconcerned
And scolding him, even as he scorned,
For bringing a slim shepherd's staff
One single blow would snap in half
And a small child's-play leather sling
To risk his feeble fortunes on
Under this feeble winter sun,
And promised him to give, that day,
His flesh to greedy birds of prey
And skulking beasts, indifferently.
But having put by shield and sword,
Naked of armor, though Saul had
Placed his own corselet on the lad
And crested helmet on his head,
David now sallied forth and stood
Against the Philistine multitude,
His round face ruddy with young blood,
And his hard shepherd years showed plain
In the hard features of his mien
As, once a brief-told prayer was done,
He shouted to their champion:
"You come to me with sword and spear,
And with you is a slave to bear

Your polished shield: behold, I come
Armed with no armor but his name,
The Lord of hosts, the living God
Of Israel, whom you have defied.
You, for your countrymen, have said
That whoso tries with you his skill,
If he be victor, you and all
The proud Philistine ranks shall come
And be as serving-men to him,
But he, in turn, if you prevail,
Shall yield his men to your control.
But I say now, before these massed
Armies drawn up face to face,
That if, henceforward, you will join
Your hearts to ours in like concern,
We and all Israel will cement
An everlasting covenant
Of peace and trust between us two,
As reason bids all bold men do,
If only your proud race forswears
Such ways as our great God abjures.
Yet if, in wrathful spite, you spurn
Our promised loves, which I have sworn,
Then I will smite you and disperse
Your unspoiled empire's boastfulness,
And give instead your flesh, this day,
To the wild beasts and birds of prey,
That all earth may remember well
There is a God in Israel.

Let this whole wide assemblage hear
That God saves not by sword or spear;
He gathers his own instruments
Through whom to wreak his veiled intents,
And if you now refuse our pledge
And choose once more the bare sword's edge,
So will he scatter your defense
And cast you helpless in our hands."
Yet bold Goliath made no sound
Nor turned to seek his kinsmen's mind,
But spat again upon the ground.

Now then at length the giant rose
And came on toward where David was,
And David hastened too, and ran,
His sling held fast in his right hand,
To meet the approaching champion,
And as he ran, contrived to reach
Into his ready shepherd's pouch,
Where lay five water-polished stones
Gathered against this looked-for chance
Out of a brook that flowed near by,
And as he still pursued his way
From it expertly chose and took
One of those smooth stones from the brook
And fitted it, yet on the run,
Into his sturdy leather sling.
And as the armies waited still,
Not knowing that it was God's will

He should deliver Israel,
The soldiers joked, on his own side,
And his three brothers, too, decried
His prowess, who then served their turn
In the front rank of King Saul's men,
Taking for proud temerity
The urge that made him risk this try,
When they now saw him take his stand
Upon a stretch of level ground
And lift the sling and whirl it round.
But most of all upon the field
Swarthy Goliath mocked and railed,
Whose hairy arms and towering form
Loomed in the valley between him
And the close-massed Philistine line.
Then David, with a short swift move,
Loosed the sling and deftly hove
The single small stone with such force
It spun across the shortening space
And smote him, even before he knew
What the boy did, upon the brow
Just over the wide eyebrows' bow,
And straight it sunk through the thin bone
And the Philistine toppled down,
Clumsily falling on his face
Among the trampled brown field grass.
Now David's hand held yet no sword,
Quickly therefore he ran and stood
Upon the unstirring giant's form

And drew the sword that was on him,
And, doubting still that he was dead,
Struck off the frowning dust-marred head.
And seeing what the stripling lad
Accomplished, the Philistines fled.
Then all those ranks of Israel
And Judah, who first judged him ill,
With jarring shout and curse and yell
Rose up and followed the fled host,
Now vanished in their own dense dust,
Till sight of both of them was lost.

But David quietly stood there
Watching the armies disappear,
A sharp wind ruffling his thick hair,
And the Lord's hand abode on him
As, thoughtful, he looked after them
And prophesied in the Lord's name:
"You fearless sons of Israel,
And you, brave Judah's sons, as well,
Could you not stop one hour with me
To question what our course shall be?
Is God so eager to release
Us from our foemen's strategies
That, by a single lucky stroke,
He should undo our long ill luck?
Only when Israel, to a man,
When Judah, sees what we have done
Not as our doing, but as his

Who is the Lord of victories,
Shall we at length cast off this shame
Our heedless lusts have yoked us in,
Avenge our pride beneath the sun
And seize the victory he has won."

And David took the head of him
He slew, and praising the Lord's name,
Bore it off to Jerusalem.

Did you sigh, my Lord,
As a slim young prince
At the promise denied
Your proud innocence
When you newly descried,
With sight opened fresh,
How heavily age
Hung its yoke on the flesh;
How the rancor and shame
Of the lame and the ill
Spelled as sure defeat
For the high as the small?
Did you sigh, my Lord,
When you saw in surprise
How the hand of decay
Warped the world to its wish;
How the rigors of death
Waited silent beneath
To confound your conceit
And deprive you of faith,
When desiring was done
— Compassionate One?

Yes, I sighed, my son,
When I saw that day
What was veiled before
From my hindered eye;

For my thought knew yet
No escape from despair,
From the harrowing hurt
All flesh passes through.
But I saw, my son,
In my swelling doubt
A homeless monk
With unshod feet,
And the glow of the peace
That shone on his face
As I watched him, plunged
In the night of my grief,
For a moment's space
Gave sorrow relief
And affirmed me a faith
In the easing of woe.

2

Did you weep, my Lord,
As a young man should
When in princely clothes
You stood by the bed
For a last brief look
At the sleeping child
Whose promise of joy
Your parting denied?
Did you weep, my Lord,
In the calm of night,
To gaze on the wife

You would leave behind?
Did you doubt the quest
That had cheated her life,
As your chariot sped
At the bidding of fate
Where no hope of love
Or delight could remain,
Where decision must fight
Its way, alone,
Till error was fled
And desiring was done
And sorrow destroyed
— Compassionate One?

Yes, I wept, my son,
To look down on them,
To recall the bliss
My hope had forgone,
To picture the hours
Of delight and ease
That had bound us in love
In our father's home;
And I burned in my heart
For the hurt I had done
To her who had never
Caused me ill.
But a voice, my son,
From the depths of pain
Bade the mind rejoice

41

Though the heart despair,
For the flow of my will
Should never abate
Till the stab of all hurt
Had found a cure,
Till I knew, of myself,
That never again
Need a man bear the weight
Of comfortless woe.

3

Did you smile, my Lord,
In the heart of peace
As you sat with your back
To the great Bo-tree
And watched how the Temptress
Came and stood,
In the shameless grace
Of her majesty,
Braving the flame
Of your swerveless glance
To wring the fee
She had thought to win,
And saw how she fled
At the flash of your wrath?
Did you smile, my Lord,
In Nirvana's dawn,
As the daystar of truth
Rose higher and higher,

And obedient in will
To your mind's intent
You traced the design
Of the subtle laws
That dispose the flow
Of effect from cause;
When your mind and your heart
And your life and your hope
Fused all in one
In a quick, new shape
As the thrust of your sure
Sharp questionings
Pierced straight down
To the deep of things?

Yes, I smiled, my son,
For at last I knew
That the doubt and defeat
Of a life were done,
And I saw that the urge
That goaded me on
Would free even those
I had wronged or hurt;
And I yearned with a sudden
Passionate thirst
To reveal what I knew
To be true and just,
To tell men's faith
That the cure of pain

Was in quenching desire
With the taste of truth,
That the age-old trust
In a walled-in self
Was a shame and a snare
And a cursedness;
And I swore, my son,
With a swerveless oath
To float no more
In the seizing bliss
That my dream and my doom
Had dowered me with,
But to rise and tell
To ailing men
The source of ill
And the healing of pain.

4

Did you laugh, my Lord,
When at length you saw
That the toil and the sweat
Of your life were through;
That the tainted food
The butcher brought
As his simple votive
Gift for you
Was the hidden means
That fate had wrought
To speed a final

Full release,
When your strength was spent
And your fight was won
And desiring was done
—Compassionate One?

Yes, I laughed, my son,
As the guileless man
Brought me the food
When my hour had come,
For I knew the vision
That guided me
Stood on the verge
Of a certainty.
But I laughed again,
With a heartier laugh,
As I saw once more
With my dying eyes
—In a way that was new
To the bent of my thought —
What long before
I had spelled out clear,
When without a word
To the wondering throng,
I lifted the golden
Lotus flower:
That the toil and the sweat
A man works through
To witness the saving

Path to peace,
In the sight of the wise
Are an empty show,
For the truest flower
Of his witnessing
Stems from the life
It is rooted in.
And so, as I lay,
On the day that I died,
The thrice blessed day,
With my friends at my side,
On the low-spread couch,
Fully quit of my pride,
I asked them to shun
Deluding tears
Lest fondness swerve
Their purposes,
And I bade them honor
My going hence,
In faithful witness
To my peace,
By striving in strength
And with diligence
For the working out
Of their own release.

INDIA'S FACE

DEAR KARL SHAPIRO:
Somewhat to my surprise
But more, sir, to my sorrow,
In a fashionable weekly
That lately caught my eyes
I fell on your pungent verses
Painting, not too unfairly,
In forthright Yankee wise,
The dark, oppressive cast
Of India's ancient face:
Her poor, her crows, her women,
Her beggars, brazening
In season, out of season,
Their cowed, submissive whine;
The gods on her looming temples
Where sculptures twine and start;
And — doubtless unaware
Of probing hidden hurt —
Her lost untouchables,
Stepchildren of her plight,
Yoked for unspeaking ages
To a penitential lot;
Then finally, for good measure,
Eking the picture out
— As if no sense could be made
Of a whole subcontinent —
The perilous lack of reason

47

That warped her mode of thought,
And the devout fanatic
Who shot her best-loved saint.

Now, as a sworn defender
Of balance everywhere
And one as quick to frown
Should some outsider dare
— However well-intentioned
And purged of easy scorn —
To pass upon our customs,
Our likings and our quirks
After a few weeks' digging,
With scant corroboration,
In half a dozen Chicagos,
Hollywoods and New Yorks,
I must convey my warm
Regret, nay, irritation,
To you and less well-meaning
Scribes and photographers
Who pillory unhampered
Her personal affairs,
That leisure failed to hand you
The luck it handed me:
To trace the India glowing
Within the mystery.

Instead of sitting and staring,
In a travel bureau's thrall,

Out of a wide, high window
In the Hotel Taj Mahal,
Could you have only ventured
Beyond debauched Bombay,
Passed up Madras, New Delhi
And the touted travelers' places,
Could you have fled a borrowed
Culture's sick devices
Cooling its idle hours
With cakes and colored ices;
Leaving cart-choked streets
To tourists and diplomats,
Had you decamped from ease
To sleep on table cots,
To squat on fresh clay floors
In huddled, straw-thatched huts
Lapped by the rank green paddies
Quilting flat Bengal;
Had you surprised young workers
In palm-hid village posts
Mapping patient measures
To double last year's crops,
Or, lodged by the sacred river
At Banaras or Hardwar,
Shared the arduous quiet
Of genial monks' retreats —
Mixing, man to man,
With brown-skins, one and all,
Cheered by the kindly care

Indoors and out-of-doors
Of gentle, guile-free souls
From Comorin to Kashmir —
India would have shown you
Beneath the ragged dress,
Beneath the unforgiving
Heat and the stale distress,
The life that kept her living
A thousand fettered years;
Behind the haunting mask
Of dust and dissolution,
The undivided presence
Her being really is,
Behind the thousand facets
The everlasting face.

Oh, throngs of surly monkeys,
And crows to wreck your tea,
And cheats devoutly plying
The trade of holiness,
And temples swarmed with looseness
For anyone to see
Tangle in tropic plenty —
If what you're looking for
Is meaningful examples
To smile at or deplore.
But it is to her people,
Not elsewhere, you must go
If you would enter India's

Close fraternity,
Pierce beyond the turmoil
That stirs her outer court;
For men you will encounter
Along the teeming ways
Of childlike unpretension
And trusting, goodly eyes
That shine a speaking peace
Into the throbbing air
Betraying centuries
Of love and inwardness;
And where her women pass you,
Companioned or alone,
They float, cool apparitions
From some unearthly realm,
Ringed with a quiet meekness,
An undulating grace,
Eternally their own.

Could you have only listened
To what their eyes would say,
Swayed to what potent rhythms
Moved your answering heart,
Not as a brusque outsider
But as one honoringly
Come to partake the secret
India waits to impart,
Slowly they would have spoken
An elemental truth

That hero souls have wrung
From suffering past belief:
That where abides the evil
Too long entrenched to kill
With righteous indignation
Or frantic rebel zeal,
The single telling answer's
To face it in yourself —
Find out the matching flaw
That panders faithlessly,
However uncommitted
You boast yourself to be,
To the deep hurt around you,
And having once for all
Demolished it inside you,
Entrust the outward issue
To time and men's good will.

And should you ever wonder
What bitter hurts we bear,
Dear candid-eyed reporters
Of others' waywardness,
What wrongs we labor under
Who live so high and smartly,
So spoon-fed and secure,
The darlings of creation,
The best-loved brood of fate,
Speak to a stumbling Negro
And, if you've paused to hear

The substance of this matter,
He will elucidate
The hard conclusion of it,
With a slow shrug suggesting
To all with wit to see
The witlessness of blaming,
Before your beam's cast out,
The corresponding mote
In India's troubled eye.

— Or so it seems to one
Who still presumes to be
Your well-wisher,

JOHN MOFFITT

September 28, 1956

III

SOMETHING IS MISSING

That neat-dressed little man
In the haberdashery store,
With the close-clipped moustache
And the nervous, rapid-fire
Flow of compulsive talk,
Is gone. Last Wednesday morning
Before he came downstairs,
A heaviness gave him warning
Things weren't working quite
The way they should; and instead
Of forcing himself to go on,
Thinking he'd open up late,
He simply went back to bed
And lay there wondering
If anything could be wrong.
Scarcely ten minutes passed
When a terror rose in his throat;
His heart, with a hollow thump,
Fumbled, missed a beat;
He sat up all in a sweat
And clutched the sheet,
And gave a slight cough and was **dead**.

Now that the first few shattered
Days are safely through
And everything that mattered
Is tumbled into the past,

And there's nothing better to do
Than keep oneself alive,
His wispy wife has opened
The shelf-lined shop again,
The shirts piled on the counters
And the prices marked down.
Hunched and empty-eyed,
She watches from her seat
Behind the register,
Her cheeks a bit more sallow,
Her hair a bit less neat,
Carefully telling each
Inquiring customer
Just how her husband died.

But though the new salesman speaks
In a soft, deliberate tone
That never makes you wonder
Why in the world you dropped in,
And though the prices make
Your buying much easier,
Something is missing without
That irrepressible man.
And slowly it comes to you
That the busy flow of talk
Was worth the time it cost;
You simply couldn't value
It right until it was missed;
For the same exasperations

That raised your bile before,
Now that he won't be back
Are the spice you look for first
On walking into the store —
Being all that a person needed
To make things feel secure.

THE APPOINTMENT

One aimless afternoon, as I
Was threading the deep woods alone,
Scanning the variegated moss
Where it encrusted, curiously,
With rich brocade the outcropped stone,
I noted with some vexèdness
That a small fly had stolen a ride
Upon my sweaty, bare forearm.

But though I brushed it from its place
Time and again, when I espied
It was a harmless forest thing
— Not a deer fly or other rash
Predator to be flicked aside —
I let it sit there, wondering
How long my passenger would choose
To stay.
         And, lengthening my stride
As I began the long walk home,
I found it still, to my surprise,
Each time a branch-end swept it clear,
Returning to my outstretched arm
As if some strange relatedness
Made it, henceforth, my copartner
Through life.
         I even pictured it
Following me, on future days,

When I went out to take the air
In pasture, field or wooded lot;
And so by slow degrees returned
To my own house, where, as the door
Was standing open just a bit,
My rider passed in unalarmed,
Confirming the fond prophecy
That somehow we were joined by fate.

But as the air about it dimmed,
The tenuous bond it felt for me
Yielded to love of daylight — when,
As to the nearest window frame
The fly streaked upward instantly,
A spider, lightly leaping down,
Stung it, wrapped it up in floss,
And stowed it for a hungry day.

SUNDAY IN THE GRAVEYARD

Out of sunlit morning, enter now
Through angel-wing iron gates,
Quietly enter with your other self
Into these sun-patterned distances
Of silent tombstones, gray-white in the green,
Into this vacant world that, as you pause,
Seems to invoke a larger, more pervasive
Peace than Sunday's.

       Here among these worn
Markers, which remind of nothing nearer
Than the question time has never answered,
And so cannot with any gesture cheat
The eye or the mind's eye of its continuing
Presence — here, under massed elms
And maples and dark spruces, which stretch on
Infinitely toward farther distances,
Move forward, now, with that one other who
— While yet you wander through the limits of
Your island universe —
Among all others, lets you most
Open yourself and say out what you are,
And as you share this early walk together
Pilots you easily through sheltered spaces
Whose intermittent play of shade and light,
Half-promise and refusal, now corrects,
Now sharpens the surrounding scene.

And while,
Screened from direct morning, you explore
The plain unfolding of bereaved men's loves,
Simply enacted by these pots
Of red geraniums,
These irises and roses, these half wasted
Remnants of last week's memorial wreaths
— By little flags officially remembered
For heroes of dead wars, where no new grieving
Tends the grassy graves, by the grouped slabs
Flanking a family vault — see unfold, too,
Men's hidden loves for those they still possess,
The unsaid faith that, though confessed but yearly,
Points a more telling index of concern
Than any witnessed weekly, out of habit,
At a marble altar.
Here, on this
Sun-bordered island washed by the wide sweep
Of time, this web of distances and arching
Heights, cut by a crisscross of neat roads,
Move onward in firm comradeship,
Out of the ocean's beat,
Out of the sunlit world of everyday,
And when your given hour has glided past,
Stroll back, side by side, to temporary
Lodgment — which, like these plain stones,
Cannot hide with any lively gesture
Your common destination.

A LEAVETAKING

How long does the life cling
To a root-severed tree?

Our mountain ash, we grew
From an infirm sapling
Brought to us, on a day
More than ten years ago,
By one we honor still
For depth of constancy,
Who died soon after that —
Before the first snow fell.
But now, as destiny
Granted more scope to it
And the neat foliage
Came thicker each fresh spring,
Our owning of it turned
Into a privilege —
So lush and heartening
Its habit was. We learned
To picture him we lost
As somehow lodged among
The boughs, for we felt his
Near presence as each gust
Of wind went whispering
Through their slim shapeliness.
And when, last May, the first
Frail blossoms opened through

Their sheath, and after them
Bright orange berries graced
The branch-end, though but few,
And so fulfilled his scheme,
It was as if the known
Spirit looked out anew —
And we forgave the past.

August had gone, when one
Midday the sky's flat blue
Was quickly overcast
And a high, tearing storm
Bore its freakish way
Up from the livid south
Across our sheltered lawn,
Till blackness swamped the sky
And the gale's hissing breath,
Close as the voice of doom,
Warned us to turn and shy
Out of its reckless track
Till quieter times should come.
And three whole days went by
Before we ventured back
To where the ash tree throve,
When, as we passed along
The border where it stood,
We found its fine-notched leaves
Hanging less lively strong
Than formerly they showed.

But though we watered it,
Soaking the leaves to bring
Its wilted forces round,
No leaf revived; too late
We saw the wind had wrung
Its taproot at the ground.

Yet one full week the life
Proved strangely loath to go
Out of leaf, twig and limb;
But then, almost as if
Some summons told it to,
The life left even its stem.
And, as we lifted our
Tree from its garden row,
It seemed as if the one
Whom we had pictured there
Himself at last withdrew,
Leaving us alone.

ARE ROSES, SYRINGAS . . .

Are roses, syringas, your desire?
Come, here are more
Than sense can take — crisp roses, folding back
From the thick bud,
White, salmon and black red,
Loaded with maddening scent
That eats along the nostrils to the brain
Till you are roughly seized and won;
Gold-eyed white syringas, too,
Hung on stiff stems, promise of lasting peace,
Like a clear fountain-burst of virginal rain:
Is there anything more that earth or sky
Or art of human hand or mind can offer
Your young desire?
Ask for it all. All, all I'll give, and more
Than ever you could ask;
Smother you with bright sprays
Of unresponding loveliness.

But is it more than this
You seek — an open smile, a kiss,
Promise of comradeship precise and virginal
As clear syringa or white rose?
No, do not ask for these:
Why ask for sure love? Why
Entreat that ultimate joy
Men were not made for, gods alone being meant

To turn it to employ?
That wasting mockery, why seek peace there?
Why want this blessedness
That needs a grace outside your own devising
To come by and possess?

Oh, be instead whatever
You would have your blessing be:
I tell you, go
Break faith with this desire
That waits to throttle you
With griping madness more than you can bear;
Ask no love anywhere —
Be, be what you require,
And of this gift weave fair
Your fragrance through time's troubled air;
Look not for love, which, even if it could be,
Must prick or fade, and wither utterly.

But if roses, if syringas are
Your best desire,
Take them — for these I'll give
More than your staggered sense can bear.

CASTAWAY

To me, handled here each day
By this changing sea in a changing way,
Sometimes it seems,
While the deep-sprung waves' lurch and shove
Whirl my lashed raft precariously
Or steer it on along a steady track,
That one chance only, among all that press on me —
Bright rush of sun on breaking
Surf, or suck of waters underneath
A comber's crest, or pause of movement in uneasy calm;
Ruddy green of massed sea-wrack,
Or flying fishes breaking from
The troughs of waves, or blown crest-foam
— One only, of all such as these,
Somewhere waits for me
Urgent enough to catch and hold my eye.

When the ultimate storm dislodges me
From my safe place and hurls me, stripped,
Among the porpoises and following sharks,
And I strike out with bold arm-strokes
As if to master yet
All that wide reach of waters that encircles me,
And then at length, my whole strength spent,
Lean back upon a wave and, eyes half-closed,
Sink gradually toward the huge deep
— Why, then the chance of dying and of death,

The glittering ecstasy that tears
Whatever was
From what still is and what must be:
That single chance, among the many that press round,
Shall with its final thrust
Tower till I cannot wrest my eyes away.

TAKE HEART

"Things were different when men felt their programme
 In the bones and pulse, not only in the brain,
Born to a trade, a belief, a set of affections;
 That instinct for belief may sprout again,
There are some who have never lost it
 And some who foster or force it into growth,
But most of us lack the right discontent, contented
 Merely to cavil. Spiritual sloth
Creeps like lichen or ivy over the hinges
 Of the doors which never move . . ."
                    — LOUIS MACNEICE, "Autumn Journal"

Who says most modern men
Feel nothing in the bones and pulse,
But only in the brain?
Take heart: are poets all?
Are none but the articulate, men?
Do not the voiceless feel
Deep in their pulse and bones
The same sure urge to plunge
Clean to the world's core?
Is it, that urge, not here
In me — and if in me,
Not in all men, somewhere?
By Jesus, it is there;
For the same pulse beat on
As lively and as warm
In each age heretofore,
Though Jeremiahs even then

Pronounced it dead and gone.
The lichen or the ivy cape,
Shroud though it may or strain
The surface of the wall
That frames the grudging door,
Could not so broadly spread
Without the ordered stones.
Nothing that was, is dead:
That lucid stuff remains,
As lively and as sure.
Scrape off the lichen, tear
The ivy cape away,
And bare the breathing rock —
The living, laughing fire
Within the breathing bones —
Capture the pulse once more
Whose hardy, measured shock
Hammers within all men,
Witnessing to the wide dark
That all is safe. Take heart:
No promise yet has failed,
No vision shone in vain.
The weighted future lives
Prisoned inside men's bones;
And the charged past, as well,
Whole, not in part,
Now in full fervor pours
Along men's straining veins
And only waits sufficient stab
To bleed it forth again.

IV

ADAM'S CHOICE

In the dark jungles where men preyed
On animal, fish, frog and bird
Or sought from tuber, fruit and nut
Their seasonal, slim livelihood,
When first a man made conscious choice
Between known and new-fashioned ways
And the incalculable scroll
Of our slow history's labored tale
Began perceptibly to unroll —
What was the fertile incident
That sired that unobserved event?
Was the clean cut a split rock piece
Inflicted on his startled flesh;
The wonder and excitement when
He first felt a bowed stick unbend
As he removed his forcing hand;
The fresh flame that he captured, where
Dead branches rubbed in windy air
Or lightning set some tree afire —
Was such, or such, or such the source
From which flowed our long history's
Ever enriching store of bold
Achievement or meek servitude?
Whatever the half-blind choice was
That impulse prompted him to embrace
To ease, if by a fraction, his
Piled load of inconveniences,

Man in that dawn could never guess
What ripenings it should produce
Before time stilled his enterprise.
Nor might he judge the potency
Involved in his veiled destiny
As he beheld a hewn plank's plane
Roll smooth and sure while resting on
Two lengths of tree trunk; or how wet
Clay lumps hardened in fire's heat;
Or how a sharpened stick broke up
Caked earth for raising a prized crop
Of millet, maize or sesamum.
Yet we, now looking back at him
From this late vantage point in time,
May trace prophetic hintings in
Such rudiments of the machine
As his slow gropings fastened on.

2

Even from thought's birth there was thus
One trend of growth to guide the race,
Stemming from that first Adam's choice;
And through far eons its live strand
Wove on, persistent, toward one end,
When fertile guesses should work out
A final agent to exploit
The myriad promises of thought.
Mark, as the ultimate design
And complement of the machine,

The marvels of the man-made brain.
See how this calculating tool
With built-in memory and slide rule
For computation — which even now
Waves untold prospects into view —
Solves in a fraction of an hour
Riddles that, twenty years before,
Would have asked lifetimes to explore;
Till logic leads us to predict
Engines that will themselves detect,
At their own self-employed impulse,
Their own missteps — and so excuse
Mankind from a last source of pride,
The presumed need to check and guide
Their functionings' exactitude;
Brains that will manage, on their own,
To mend such parts as shall break down,
And hence, in future, will have learned
What projects they should take in hand,
When even invention shall become
A flourish for them to perform.
We can envision times to come
When those who have outlived the bomb
— Through agency of such genes as
Rendered their flesh impervious
To radiation and nerve gas —
Shall have devised an omniverse
Complex of cog-wheels, tubes and wires
That will provide a substitute

For every phase of human thought;
When man and his machines at last
Shall hold intelligent discourse,
And the machines, too, with their own
Kind hold terse conversation;
When nothing men must calculate
Or measure or conclude about
But can be fed to some machine
To factor and decide upon.

3

What more befitting, then, for man,
Confronted with his new machine,
Than to snatch up the challenge thrown
By this late fruit of Adam's choice
At the whole fathering human race?
For, at some juncture, time shall leave
Mankind one last alternative
To the machine's complete domain,
One final, daring human thing
Forever lost to a machine:
To set themselves perforce to unlearn
What the machine can best perform —
All those brave feats of mind and will
They boasted in the interval
Between that first dim act of choice
And the immediate time and place —
And sound the flow of consciousness
That wells from the heart's inmost space,

Beyond the realm of conscious choice,
The source of all that shines apart
In music, poetry and art,
Beyond the reach of "would" or "ought,"
The unseen orderer of thought,
Which welds in one tight-webbed design
The spirits of all living men;
And having, so, earned all that was
Required of them by way of choice,
Bear witness to their inward grace,
Attuned to move and breathe and feel
In the clear vision of the real,
Watching the curious, long-drawn scroll
Man's history labors to unroll,
Not as mere cogs within the scheme
But as souls unconstrained by time
Who bear the burden of "I am"
And, waiting for time's stop to come,
Embrace the arduous interim.

Date Due